Traditional Salt Dough

Traditional
Salt Dough

PRACTICAL PROJECTS TO DECORATE THE HOME

Cheryl Owen

LORENZ BOOKS

First published in 1999 by Lorenz Books

© Anness Publishing Limited 1999

Lorenz Books is an imprint of
Anness Publishing Limited
Hermes House
88–89 Blackfriars Road
London SE1 8HA

This edition distributed in Canada by Raincoast Books, 8680 Cambie Street, Vancouver, British Columbia V6P 6M9

ISBN 0 7548 0275 2

A CIP catalogue record for this book
is available from the British Library

Publisher: Joanna Lorenz
Project editor: Simona Hill
Designer: Bobbie Colgate-Stone
Editorial reader: Joy Wotton

Printed and bound in Singapore

1 3 5 7 9 10 8 6 4 2

ACKNOWLEDGEMENTS
The publishers would like to thank the following project makers:
Penny Boylan for the Country Hearts Garland; Petra Boase for the Valentine's Box; Lucinda Ganderton for the
Braided Candle Holder, Checkered Heart, Flying Angel, Fruit-filled Cornucopia, Gingerbread Heart, Mexican Tree of Life,
Sponged Goose Keyrack and Traditional Wheatsheaf; Alison Jenkins for the Goddess Wall Plaque; Cheryl Owen for the Court Jester,
Fish Plaque, Jewelled Window Ornaments, Nutcracker Soldier, Shaker Hand, Sun Plaque, Traditional Folk Angel and Tree Plaques;
Ann Zwemmer for the Indian-style Ornaments

Thanks to the following photographers:
Madeleine Brehaut, Rodney Forte, Debbie Patterson, Graham Rae and Steve Tanner

Contents

Introduction

♥

THE TECHNIQUE OF MODELLING DOUGH, which has obvious connections with bread-making, has been known for many centuries: the ancient Egyptians, Greeks and Romans all used it to make religious offerings. It became very popular as a decorative craft in nineteenth-century Germany, when salt was first added to the dough to prevent finished ornaments from being nibbled by mice. It's also a thriving and exuberant folk-art tradition in South America. The projects in this book reflect these cultural roots, concentrating on traditional designs and decorations.

Salt dough is cheap and easy to make: all you need is plain (all-purpose) flour, salt and water. You probably have most of the equipment you'll need to make, shape and decorate it in your kitchen already. Pastry moulds and cutters are easy to use and make very satisfying shapes.

Bake the models in a very cool oven to prevent the dough from cracking, and make sure that they are completely hard all over before leaving them to cool. You can tint or marble the dough before you shape it, paint it after baking with subtle watercolours or vibrant acrylics, sponge it, gild it or leave it plain, but always protect your finished creations with several coats of varnish.

Making and Using Salt Dough

Detailed instructions are given for making each project in this book, but in this section you'll find some useful general tips to help you prepare, mould and decorate the dough effectively.

MAKING THE DOUGH

The basic recipe is easy to remember, and you will soon learn to recognize the consistency you need for a pliable dough.

YOU WILL NEED
- *2 cups plain (all-purpose) flour*
- *1 cup salt*
- *1 cup tepid water*

ROLLING OUT

1 Roll out the dough on a flat, lightly floured surface. Dust the rolling pin very lightly with flour if it begins to stick. Alternatively, roll the dough on a sheet of non-stick baking parchment, so that the whole thing can be lifted with the minimum of disturbance on to a baking tray for drying in the oven.

1 Mix the flour and salt in a bowl. Add about half of the water. Mix with a wooden spoon, gradually adding more water until the dough is firm but not too wet. If it becomes too sticky, add more flour to achieve a firm texture.

2 Turn the dough out on to a work surface. If you need to increase the quantities for a large project, it is easier to mix the dough in several batches.

3 With floured hands, knead the dough thoroughly for at least 10 minutes to achieve an elastic consistency. Allow the dough to rest for 30 minutes in a plastic bag.

4 Unused dough can be stored in the fridge for 2–3 days. If it becomes wet and sticky, add more flour and knead very thoroughly until smooth and elastic. Old or wet dough is too stretchy and will not keep its shape.

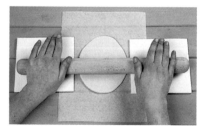

2 For flat items, use rolling guides such as two ceramic tiles to help you achieve an even thickness: place the tiles at each side of the dough for the rolling pin to rest on.

MAKING AND USING TEMPLATES

1 Templates for all the projects are given at the back of the book. Enlarge the designs if necessary by scaling them up on graph paper or using the enlargement facility on a photocopier. Templates can be cut out of paper, cardboard or baking parchment (which has the advantage of being transparent).

2 Place the template on the rolled-out dough and cut around it using a sharp knife. Remove the excess dough, then work around the shape, trimming away rough edges and tidying curves. Gently pat the edges of the shape with your finger or the flat of a knife blade to create a rounded edge.

3 Details can be transferred by replacing the template and pricking through the design with a pin. After removing the template, the pricked image can be enhanced by joining the dots with the point of a toothpick or the tip of a knife blade.

WORKING WITH MOULDS AND ARMATURES

1 An ovenproof bowl or plate can be used as a mould. Always coat it with cooking oil so that the model will release easily once baked. Use a drier dough than usual, to prevent it from stretching or tearing, and roll it to a thickness of 8mm/⅜in. Lift the rolled dough carefully into place and smooth it around the mould with your hands.

2 When making solid shapes, the dough needs to be moulded over an armature to give it a firm structure and to shorten the drying time. Sturdy cardboard can be used, as can anything that is ovenproof at low temperatures. Cover the cardboard shape with aluminium foil, then spread the salt dough around the armature.

EMBOSSING AND EMBEDDING

1 Dough can be textured with embossing tools. Experiment on spare dough until you find a texture suitable for the model you are making. Try using a fork, knife, comb or corrugated cardboard. Ready-made embossing tools, used for cake decorating, are excellent.

2 Decorative materials, such as shells, glass, fireproof beads, mosaic tiles and broken china, can be embedded in the dough. Press the object into the dough and smooth the edge with a moistened finger. If you plan to hang up the item, embed a loop of wire in the back before baking.

BAKING THE DOUGH

1 Dry out the moulded dough on a baking tray lined with non-stick baking parchment placed on a low shelf in the oven. Several models can be baked at the same time, but rotate their shelf positions to achieve even results. It is important to bake salt dough at a low temperature (120°C/250°F/Gas ½) and over a long period of time to avoid distorting, cracking or discolouring. Leave the item in the oven once it has been switched off to finish off the drying-out process. All baking times for the projects are approximate.

2 Items that are to remain unpainted can be baked at a slightly higher temperature (150°C/300°F/Gas 2) to give them a little colour. When the desired colour has been reached, turn the oven down to 120°C/250°F/Gas ½ and place them on the lowest shelf to continue drying out.

3 Large flat pieces can be weighted down after at least 3 hours' baking, to keep them flat. Place an ovenproof plate or similar weight on top of the item, making sure that the weight is evenly distributed, and return to the oven to finish baking.

SMOOTHING THE EDGES

After baking, rough edges and burrs can be smoothed off quickly and easily using a metal nail file or fine sandpaper.

DECORATING

1 Prepare the baked salt dough for decorating by priming with several coats of acrylic gesso. If this is unavailable, you can also use matt emulsion (flat latex) paint. Be careful not to obscure fine details with thick layers of paint.

2 When the primer is dry, the model can be painted with a wide variety of paints. Acrylic gouache works particularly well on salt dough, but watercolour inks, metallic paints and sprays all create different effects.

3 Salt dough needs many coats of acrylic or polyurethane varnish to protect the surface from dust and moisture. (Salt dough will not survive in a damp atmosphere, and it cannot be used for items that hold water.) Models must be absolutely dry before varnishing. Allow the paint to dry for at least 6 hours, then apply at least four coats of varnish.

Hearts and Hands

♥

UNIVERSALLY RECOGNIZED as the symbol of divine and
earthly love, the heart motif is common to many folk
cultures and has historically been used to decorate costumes,
furnishings and household objects. The Scandinavians
were particularly fond of the heart and a red heart
is still one of the most popular Danish Christmas
decorations today. Like the heart, the Healing Hand is a
simple yet powerful motif - it is an ancient symbol of
friendship and giving. Use the projects in this chapter to
make special, from-the-heart gifts such as the tiny, decorated
Valentine's Box or the Shaker Hand.

Shaker Hand

Make a special souvenir of a friend or relative by drawing around their hand and preserving the outline in salt dough. The bordered heart motif is typical of traditional Shaker style, and is often found in nineteenth-century punched metal designs.

You will need
- *salt dough*
- *rolling pin*
- *baking parchment*
- *knitting needle*
- *small, sharp knife*
- *heart-shaped cookie cutter (optional)*
- *brass eyelet*
- *modelling tool (optional)*
- *tin-tacks (metal tacks)*
- *baking tray*
- *acrylic matt (flat) varnish*
- *varnishing brush*

1 Roll out the dough on a sheet of baking parchment to a thickness of 1.5cm/⅝in. Lay a hand flat on the dough with the fingers together. Use a knitting needle to trace around the edge and mark the fingers, then cut out the hand outline using a sharp knife. Round the cut edges with a moistened finger.

2 Cut out a heart from the palm, either cutting freehand with a small knife or using a heart-shaped cutter. Turn the hand over and insert a brass eyelet to form a hanger.

3 Use a modelling tool or the tip of a knife blade to mark the fingers. Press tin-tacks into the dough to outline the cut-out heart. Transfer the hand, on the baking parchment, to a baking tray and bake at 120°C/250°F/Gas ½ for 9 hours. Allow to cool, then apply 5 coats of varnish, allowing the varnish to dry thoroughly between each coat.

Gingerbread Heart

Based on traditional German gingerbread, this folk-art heart should be decorated in bright colours.

YOU WILL NEED
- ♦ *paper and pencil for template*
- ♦ *scissors*
- ♦ *salt dough*
- ♦ *rolling pin*
- ♦ *baking parchment*
- ♦ *small, sharp knife*
- ♦ *aspic or jelly cutters for the small shapes*
- ♦ *brass eyelet*
- ♦ *acrylic gesso*
- ♦ *medium and fine paintbrushes*
- ♦ *acrylic or craft paints*
- ♦ *acrylic matt (flat) varnish*
- ♦ *40cm/16in length of paper ribbon*

1 Make a heart template. Roll out the dough on parchment 8mm/ ⅜in thick. Cut out the heart. Cut small shapes for decoration and stick in place. Add an eyelet for hanging.

2 Bake the dough for 9 hours. Allow to cool, then prime with acrylic gesso. Paint as desired, then varnish. Thread paper ribbon through the eyelet and knot.

Checkered Hearts

These ornaments take inspiration from traditional Scandinavian folk art. The dough squares are formed by making deep indentations, though they give the impression of being separate pieces woven together.

YOU WILL NEED
- *pencil and scissors*
- *salt dough and rolling pin*
- *baking parchment*
- *small, sharp knife*
- *large pin or small skewer*
- *modelling tool (optional)*
- *gold paperclip*
- *wire cutters*
- *baking tray*
- *acrylic gesso and paintbrushes*
- *cherry red acrylic or craft paint*
- *acrylic matt (flat) varnish*
- *40cm/16in length of red raffia*

1 Trace the template and cut out. Roll out the dough on parchment 8mm/⅜in thick. Place the template on top and cut around it. Mark the squares by pricking with a pin. Trace over the pricked lines with a knife or modelling tool.

2 Cut a paperclip in half to make a hanging loop and insert in the top of the heart. Transfer to a baking tray and bake at 120°C/250°C/Gas ½ for 9 hours until hard, then leave to cool.

3 Prime the areas to be painted with acrylic gesso, then paint selected areas with red acrylic or craft paint. Apply four coats of varnish. Thread a piece of red raffia through the loop and tie the ends in a decorative bow.

Country Hearts Garland

For country-style festivities, make this lovely garland using hearts painted in traditional shades. Use scraps of homespun fabrics to trim the hearts, in keeping with the country feel – try dipping cotton ticking in tea to give it an aged look.

You will need
- *salt dough*
- *rolling pin*
- *baking parchment*
- *heart-shaped cookie cutters*
- *small, sharp knife (optional)*
- *toothpick*
- *baking tray*
- *string and large darning needle*
- *buttons, scraps of cotton fabrics, decorative twine, dried bay leaves*
- *metal nail file or fine sandpaper*
- *acrylic gesso*
- *medium and fine paintbrushes*
- *acrylic paints*
- *acrylic matt (flat) varnish*

1 Roll the salt dough 5mm/¼in thick. Cut out a heart. Make a hole in the top with a toothpick, making sure it is large enough not to close up during baking. Make enough hearts for your garland.

2 Lift the hearts on to a baking tray lined with baking parchment and bake at 120°C/250°F/Gas ½ for at least 5-6 hours, turning them over halfway through the cooking time.

3 Allow the dough to cool. Smooth any rough edges with a nail file or some fine sandpaper. Prime the hearts with two coats of acrylic gesso and leave to dry.

4 Paint both sides of each heart. When the paint is dry, protect it with four coats of varnish. Allow the varnish to dry thoroughly between each coat.

5 Thread string through each heart. Tie on buttons and scraps of homespun cotton fabrics. Thread the hearts on to twine, adding buttons, leaves and fabric as desired.

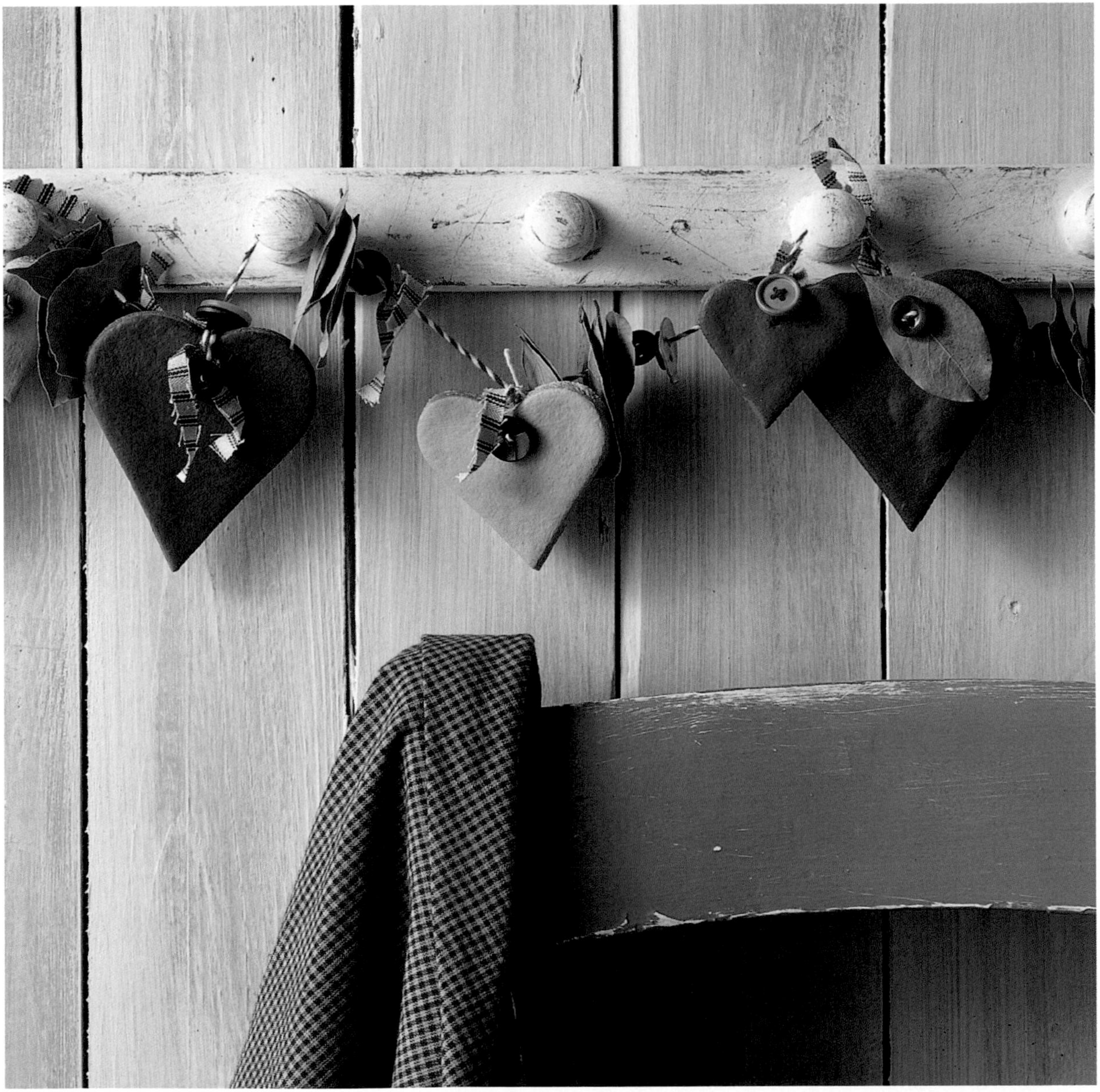

Valentine's Box

Send your sweetheart a special gift in this precious lidded box. Use a round ovenproof dish as a mould for the base. It doesn't need to have a flat bottom, as the box will stand securely on its own little feet.

YOU WILL NEED
- *salt dough*
- *rolling pin*
- *baking parchment*
- *small ovenproof dish*
- *cooking oil*
- *small, sharp knife*
- *baking tray*
- *paper, pencil and scissors or cookie cutters*
- *acrylic gesso*
- *medium and fine paintbrushes*
- *acrylic or craft paints*
- *acrylic satin (low luster) varnish*

1 Coat the outside of the ovenproof dish with oil. Roll the dough out on baking parchment to a thickness of 8mm/⅜in. Lift it over the dish and mould it to the sides, cutting away the excess dough. Smooth the dough.

2 Roll four 1.5cm/⅝in diameter balls of dough. Moisten and press gently on to the base of the bowl to make feet. Transfer to a baking tray lined with baking parchment and bake at 120°C/250°F/Gas ½ for 9 hours, until hard.

3 To make the lid, re-roll the remaining dough to a thickness of 8mm/⅜in. Cut out a circle and a heart, using your own templates or cookie cutters. Transfer the pieces to a baking tray lined with baking parchment and bake for 45 minutes.

4 Allow the pieces to cool. Blunt the end of the heart with a sharp knife, then attach it to the lid using raw dough, smoothing the joins with a moistened finger. Return the lid to the oven for 9 hours.

5 Leave the hardened dough to cool. Carefully remove the bowl from the mould. Prime the pieces with acrylic gesso and leave to dry. Decorate inside and out with acrylic or craft paints, then apply four coats of varnish to finish.

Flying Angel

This angel has charming curly hair, a cheeky smile and a heart emblazoned on his chest. Once you have mastered the basic template, you can create all sorts of delightful cherubic variations.

YOU WILL NEED
- *baking parchment*
- *pencil*
- *salt dough*
- *modelling tool*
- *large pin*
- *small heart-shaped cutter*
- *paperclip*
- *wire cutters*
- *baking tray*
- *acrylic gesso*
- *paintbrushes*
- *acrylic or craft paints*
- *acrylic matt (flat) varnish*

1 Copy the template provided on to a 20cm/8in square of baking parchment on which the angel will be assembled. First make the wings by rolling curved sausages of dough and placing them between the traced outlines. Roll a 3cm/1¼in ball of dough to form the head and flatten it slightly. Moisten the inner edge of the right wing and place the head in position.

2 Mould the body shape, moisten the top edges and join to the head and wings. Smooth the edges with a modelling tool. The angel's hair is formed from small coils of dough, of various sizes, arranged around the head. Mark the eyes and mouth with a large pin.

3 Cut out a small heart to decorate the dress. Moisten it and press into place. Make the feet from balls of dough, pressed into triangles. Snip the paperclip in half and press it into the top of the head. Bake for 10 hours. Allow to cool. Prime with acrylic gesso and leave to dry. Paint the model with acrylic or craft paints, then apply four coats of matt (flat) varnish.

Decorative Plaques

♥

DRESS UP A DULL WALL with one of these plaques. The moulded Sun Plaque is perfect for a protected outdoor spot, such as a patio or courtyard; a benevolent mascot for warm days and outdoor living. The Mexican Tree of Life is worked over a wire armature, the chirping, buzzing and slithering inhabitants being added later. Children will enjoy making their own Garland of Clowns, since the clothing and decorations – even the length of the garland – are a matter of individual choice. The Fish Plaque looks fiddly, but is in fact simple to make, and is versatile enough to use either as a plaque or a centrepiece.

Mexican Tree of Life

This wonderful model looks very complex, but is in fact quite straightforward to make. The tree itself is left unpainted to contrast with the assortment of bright flowers and exotic creatures on its branches.

YOU WILL NEED
- *medium and fine galvanized wire*
- *wire cutters*
- *narrow masking tape*
- *salt dough*
- *baking parchment*
- *small, sharp knife*
- *knitting needle and modelling tools*
- *dressmaker's glass-headed pins*
- *aluminium foil*
- *baking tray*
- *watercolour inks*
- *paintbrushes*
- *acrylic satin (low luster) and matt (flat) varnish*

1 The tree is built up over a wire armature which supports its branches during and after baking. Make this from lengths of medium-gauge galvanized wire, bound together with narrow masking tape.

2 Working on baking parchment, cover the wire armature with a layer of dough, shaping the ends of the branches into points, ensuring that the dough covers the wire completely. Smooth over the joins.

3 Form the snake from a tapered roll of dough. Cut a small mouth and insert a pea-sized apple. Mark the eye. Moisten the dough and coil the snake around the trunk. Shape leaves on fine wire, mark the veins and insert into the branches, securing with a collar of dough.

4 Build up the flowers petal by petal. Roll balls of dough, pinch them into diamond shapes and press together. Decorate the centres with small balls of dough and indent the petals with a knitting needle.

5 Make the bee and butterfly by rolling small round heads and sausage-shaped bodies. Flatten small balls of dough for the wings. Moisten and press on to the bodies. Use dressmaker's glass-headed pins as antennae.

6 Attach the flowers and insects to the tree with short wire stalks. Model the bird. Place pads of foil under the flowers to support them during baking.

7 Transfer the model, on the parchment, to a baking tray and bake at 120°C/250°F/Gas ½ for 10 hours. Allow to cool. Paint with watercolour inks, leaving the trunk unpainted. Coat the painted areas with four coats of satin varnish (low luster) and the trunk with four coats of matt (flat) varnish.

Sun Plaque

A beaming sun makes a welcoming decoration. His expressive face is created by moulding the features separately before applying them to the basic shape. The rosy cheeks and chin are sponged with colour.

YOU WILL NEED
- *18cm/7in diameter ovenproof plate*
- *sheet of hard wooden board (to fit in the oven)*
- *masking tape*
- *petroleum jelly*
- *salt dough*
- *rolling pin*
- *tracing paper*
- *pencil*
- *scissors*
- *small, sharp knife*
- *skewer*
- *acrylic gesso*
- *paintbrushes*
- *acrylic or craft paints*
- *ceramic tile (optional)*
- *sponge*
- *acrylic satin (low luster) varnish*
- *fine gold cord*

1 Invert the plate in the centre of the hard wooden board and secure with masking tape. Coat with petroleum jelly. Roll the dough into a 30cm/12in circle, 8mm/⅜in thick. Centre it over the plate.

2 Copy the templates provided on to tracing paper. Place the sun-ray template on the dough around the plate and cut out using a sharp knife. Smooth the cut edges with a moistened finger.

3 Roll a 1cm/½in thick sausage of dough 5cm/2in long for the nose. Moisten and stick in place, then stroke the top on to the face. Press two 1cm/½in balls on the sides of the nose and use the point of a pencil to form the nostrils. Use your thumbs to make eye sockets.

4 Draw around the eye templates with the tip of a knife. Roll thin sausages to outline the eyes. Roll two small balls and flatten them to make eyeballs. Cut a mouth from 5mm/¼in thick dough and place 1.5cm/⅝in below the nose. Draw the lip division with the knife tip.

5 Roll two 2cm/⅜in diameter balls for the cheeks and a 1.5cm/⅝in ball for the chin. Flatten them, then press on to the face and smooth out. Stick on thin sausages for the eyebrows. Make a hole in the top of the plaque with a skewer. Bake at 120°C/250°F/Gas ½ for 12 hours. When the face is hard, turn the plaque over and remove the plate.

6 When cool, prime the plaque with acrylic gesso, then paint with acrylic or craft paints. Add a gentle blush to the cheeks and chin using pink paint on a sponge. Leave to dry, then apply four coats of varnish. Hang up with gold cord.

Fish Plaque

This plaque will look stunning hung on a wall or used as a centrepiece. The fish swimming around the rim and the small details in the centre are all painted with watercolours for a suitably marine effect.

YOU WILL NEED
- *21cm/8½in diameter plate*
- *pencil, paper and scissors*
- *baking parchment*
- *salt dough and rolling pin*
- *small, sharp knife*
- *large needle*
- *baking tray*
- *watercolour paints*
- *paintbrushes*
- *acrylic satin (low luster) varnish*

1 Invert a plate on a sheet of baking parchment. Draw around it. Roll a dough sausage 1.5cm/⅝in thick and arrange it around the circumference of the circle, moistening the dough at joins to secure in place.

2 Roll dough sausages 5mm/¼in thick and cut into 5.5cm/2¼in lengths. Moisten the ends and press them to the plaque rim. For row two, cut sausages 4.5cm/1¾in long. For row three, 5.5cm/2¼in long and join their ends against alternate semicircles. For row four they should be 4.5cm/1¾in long, and the three centre ones 3cm/1¼in long.

3 Copy the templates provided and cut out. Roll out the dough on baking parchment to a thickness of 5mm/¼in and cut out ten large fish. Cut out five small fish and five starfish freehand. Smooth the cut edges and use a large needle to mark eyes, fins, scales and tails.

4 Mould fins from dough, moisten and press on to the fish. Transfer all the pieces, on the parchment, to a baking tray and bake for 1 hour. Cool, then moisten the undersides of the shapes, smear with dough and press on to the plaque. Bake for 10 hours. When cool, paint the plaque with watercolours and apply four coats of varnish.

Goddess Wall Plaque

This impressive plaque is built over a mould to give depth and solidity, and the three-dimensional effect is completed with the applied features. The paint effect gives the impression of a terracotta relief sculpture.

YOU WILL NEED
- *pencil, paper and scissors*
- *salt dough*
- *rolling pin*
- *small, sharp knife*
- *ovenproof saucer and aluminium foil*
- *baking tray*
- *modelling tool and toothpick*
- *terracotta matt emulsion (flat latex) paint and paintbrushes*
- *terracotta-effect textured paint*
- *acrylic paints in black and gold*
- *acrylic matt (flat) varnish*
- *gold jewellery wire*
- *picture hanger and strong glue*

1 Enlarge the template provided and cut out. Roll out the dough to a thickness of 5mm/¼in. Cut around the outline of the template using a sharp knife.

2 Cover the convex side of the saucer with foil and place on the baking tray. Place the dough shape on top. Smooth the edges. Using a modelling tool, draw the hairline, eyes, eyebrows, nose and chin.

3 Cut out the templates for the head dress, eyes, mouth and nose. Roll some dough 5mm/¼in thick and cut out all the shapes with a sharp knife. Moisten the plaque surface and stick the shapes in place. Add details with a modelling tool. Pierce the earlobes with a toothpick.

4 Roll small quantities of dough into thin tapered sausages and add eyebrows and the border of the head dress. Use small balls of dough to make the necklace and forehead decoration. Smooth out the joins with a moistened modelling tool. Bake the plaque for 12 hours.

5 Apply an undercoat of terracotta matt emulsion (flat latex) paint, then a base coat of terracotta textured paint. Pick out the features and details using paints. Apply four coats of matt (flat) varnish. Add wire loops to the ear lobes and a picture hanger to the back.

Garland of Clowns

This amusing row of clowns is easy enough for children to make. The bodies are cut out with a pastry cutter, and can be decorated as simply or as lavishly as you wish. Thread the clowns together on fine ribbons to make a garland of any length.

You will need
- ♦ *salt dough*
- ♦ *rolling pin*
- ♦ *baking parchment*
- ♦ *gingerbread-man pastry cutter*
- ♦ *large needle*
- ♦ *sieve (sifter)*
- ♦ *small, sharp knife*
- ♦ *baking tray*
- ♦ *acrylic gesso*
- ♦ *paintbrushes*
- ♦ *pigmented drawing inks*
- ♦ *acrylic matt (flat) varnish*
- ♦ *fine ribbons*

1 Roll out the dough on baking parchment to a thickness of 8mm/⅜in and cut out the clowns using a gingerbread-man cutter. Roll balls of dough for their noses, moisten and press in place. Draw the features with a large needle.

2 Pierce a hole through each hand to thread with ribbon. Press the needle across the wrists to make cuffs, and draw details such as seams and trouser bottoms. Smooth the edges with a moistened finger.

3 Roll the remaining dough to a thickness of 3mm/⅛in and cut out hats, collars, bow-ties, braces and patches. Moisten the pieces and press in place.

4 Make buttons and ears from small balls of dough, indented with a needle. For curly hair, press some dough through the mesh of a sieve (sifter), cut off the shreds and press in place.

5 For straight hair, arrange dough shapes and indent with a knife. Use very thin sausages of dough to make shoelaces. Indent stitches on the patches. Transfer the clowns, on the parchment, to a baking tray and bake for 12 hours.

6 When cool, prime with acrylic gesso. Paint the clowns with inks mixed with gesso. Apply four coats of varnish, allowing the varnish to dry between each coat. Thread the clowns on to a double length of fine ribbon.

Folk Traditions

♥

WORKING WITH SALT DOUGH used to be the "poor man's craft", since the materials were to be found in every pantry and the craft was available to everyone. It is no surprise therefore that many folk cultures have salt dough modelling in common. The motifs used in this chapter are those that have been handed down through the generations. The Traditional Wheatsheaf and Fruit-filled Cornucopia celebrate the bounty of the harvest, while the Braided Candle Holder and Folk Angel are well-loved decorations. The familiar image of a wild goose lends a touch of whimsy to the practical keyrack – a must in every home.

Traditional Wheatsheaf

The wonderful golden colour of baked dough lends itself beautifully to this classic design. Simply varnish the baked dough and add natural twine for hanging.

YOU WILL NEED
- *thin cardboard*
- *pencil*
- *scissors*
- *salt dough*
- *rolling pin*
- *baking parchment*
- *small, sharp knife*
- *modelling tools*
- *galvanized wire*
- *baking tray*
- *acrylic matt (flat) varnish*
- *paintbrush*
- *natural raffia*

1 Enlarge the template provided to a height of 25cm/10in. Transfer the outline to thin cardboard and cut out. Roll out the dough on baking parchment to 5mm/¼in thick and cut out the background shape using a sharp knife.

2 Roll small lumps of the remaining dough into thin sausages about 10cm/4in long. Moisten the background and fix on the stalks, easing them into place with a modelling tool. Leave a gap of about 2cm/¾in for the tie, then add another section of stalks.

3 To mould an ear of corn, start by making a flat pad of dough about 4 x 1cm/1½ x ½in. Use a flat-ended modelling tool to press a chevron pattern along the centre of the ear.

4 Trim away the end of each section of the ear and smooth into a curve with a modelling tool. Repeat to make enough ears to fill the top of the wheatsheaf.

5 Attach the ears in three rows. Push a wire loop into the back of the sheaf to make a hanger. Bake at 150°C/300°F/Gas 2 until lightly coloured. Turn the oven down and bake until dry and hard.

6 When cool, apply four coats of varnish on both sides, leaving it to dry between coats. Cut a bundle of natural raffia to a length of 50cm/20in and tie in a reef knot around the centre of the wheatsheaf. Trim the ends.

Fruit-filled Cornucopia

A wealth of dusky, painted fruit appears to burst from the natural dough base of this harvest cornucopia.

You will need
- *paper*
- *pencil*
- *salt dough*
- *rolling pin*
- *baking parchment*
- *small, sharp knife*
- *dressmaker's pin*
- *modelling tool*
- *knitting needle*
- *2 cloves*
- *brass eyelet*
- *baking tray*
- *watercolour inks*
- *paintbrushes*
- *acrylic matt (flat) varnish*

1 Copy the template provided and cut out. Roll out the dough on baking parchment to 8mm/⅜in thick. Place the template on the dough, cut around it, then transfer the pattern by pricking with a pin. Define the ridges of the shell.

2 Shape a pear, plum and apple from the remaining dough. Moisten the undersides and press into place. Shape and add the leaves in the same way. Mark the veins with the tip of a knife.

3 Roll small balls for grapes and elongate them slightly. Make blackberries by pressing pellets of dough on to 8mm/⅜in foundation balls. Make the cherries and nuts from dough balls indented with a knitting needle. Make the redcurrants and mark each with a cross.

4 Form 2cm/¾in balls of dough into a conical shape for strawberries and add a stalk to the top. Mark the seeds with a needle. Moisten and press into position. Add stalks to the cherries, apple, plum and pear. Insert cloves into the bases of the apple and pear.

5 Cut out four more leaves and attach to the underside of the cornucopia. Press an eyelet into the back for hanging. Transfer the model to a baking tray and bake for 20 hours. When cool, paint with watercolour inks. Apply four coats of matt (flat) varnish.

Sponged Goose Keyrack

This colourful keyrack makes a pretty, rustic wall decoration as well as being a practical place to keep household keys. The natural "feathered" effect is created by stippling and sponging on the colour.

YOU WILL NEED
- *tracing paper*
- *pencil*
- *scissors*
- *salt dough*
- *rolling pin*
- *baking parchment*
- *small, sharp knife*
- *dressmaker's pin*
- *modelling tool*
- *glass toy eye or black bead*
- *4 small brass hooks*
- *2 brass eyelets*
- *baking tray*
- *acrylic gesso*
- *paintbrushes*
- *acrylic or craft paints*
- *natural sponge*
- *acrylic matt (flat) varnish*
- *picture wire*

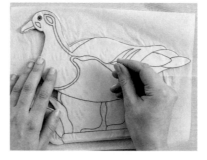

1 Enlarge the template provided and cut out of tracing paper. Roll out the dough on baking parchment to a thickness of 1cm/½in. Cut around the template and transfer the details by pricking with a pin. Smooth the cut edges, then use a modelling tool to define the lines on the wings and body. Press the eye into place.

2 Roll a 15 x 1cm/6 x ½in sausage from the remaining dough, moisten it and attach to the lower edge of the model. Use a modelling tool to mark the reeds. Push four hooks into this supporting roll, as marked on the template. Transfer the model, on the parchment, to a baking tray and bake for 2 hours. Remove from the oven and insert two brass eyelets into the back. Bake for another 10 hours. Allow to cool.

3 Prime the whole model with acrylic gesso. When dry, apply stippled and sponged colour using a dry brush and a small natural sponge. Leave to dry, then apply four coats of matt (flat) varnish. Fix a length of wire between the eyelets on the back for hanging.

Braided Candle Holder

This candle holder has a charming rustic feel and is made with interwoven braids of dough forming a circular base. It is finished simply with a few coats of varnish to retain the natural colour of the dough.

YOU WILL NEED
- *shallow 15cm/6in diameter oven-proof dish with wide rim, lined with baking parchment*
- *salt dough*
- *rolling pin*
- *6cm/2½in round pastry cutter*
- *small, sharp knife*
- *modelling tool*
- *acrylic matt (flat) varnish*
- *paintbrush*

1 Roll out the dough and cut a circular foundation. Roll most of the remaining dough into thin sausages. Cut into 15cm/6in lengths. Arrange 32 around the circle, leaving space for a candle.

2 Working in pairs, weave the lengths of dough by placing each alternate roll over the one next to it. Work all around the dish and repeat twice to form a braid.

3 Trim the end of each roll and tuck under to form a neat rim. Make the candleholder from two rings of dough placed one on top of the other. Bake the dough at 150°C/300°F/Gas 2 until lightly coloured, then turn the oven down and leave to dry out. Apply four coats of matt (flat) varnish.

Traditional Folk Angel

A heralding angel is a familiar symbol of American folk art. This charming example makes a delightful housewarming gift. The angel is created from a single flat piece of dough, so it will bake evenly.

YOU WILL NEED
- *salt dough*
- *rolling pin*
- *baking parchment*
- *pencil*
- *scissors*
- *small, sharp knife*
- *dressmaker's pin*
- *paperclip*
- *wire cutters*
- *baking tray*
- *watercolour paints*
- *paintbrushes*
- *acrylic matt (flat) varnish*
- *coloured string or fine ribbon*

1 Roll out the dough on baking parchment to 1cm/½in thick. Enlarge the template provided and cut it out of parchment. Place on the dough and cut out the shape. Transfer the design details by pricking with a pin. Trace along the lines with a knife to make indentations.

2 Cut a paperclip in half and insert the two loops into the cut edges leaving the loops just visible as shown. Transfer the angel, on the parchment, to a baking tray and bake at 120°C/250°F/Gas ½ for 10 hours. Allow to cool.

3 Paint the model with watercolour paints, applying the paint thinly. Leave the flesh areas unpainted, but tint the cheek with a little pink. When dry, apply four coats of varnish. Hang the angel on coloured string or fine ribbon.

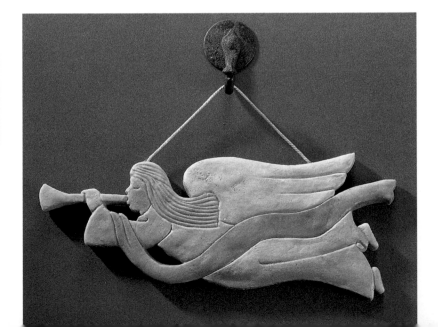

Festivities

THE ADVENT OF CHRISTMAS brings with it the urge to create new and colourful decorations. Somehow we tire of Christmas ornaments as children tire of toys, and we are always ready for new and exciting replacements! Make these projects in good time, and you may have some extra to give away. Hang the Jewelled Window Ornaments near light and see them sparkle; display bright Indian-style decorations on a window-sill or create unusual tree decorations on an animal theme. Make a child smile with the Nutcracker Soldier, whose arms actually move, or the gentle Court Jester, who will dance and loll his head for an appreciative audience.

Jewelled Window Ornaments

These stylish decorations catch the light beautifully when hung in front of a window. The wonderful stained-glass effect in the centre of the models is created using melted boiled sweets (candies).

You will need
♦ *paper*
♦ *pencil*
♦ *scissors*
♦ *salt dough*
♦ *rolling pin*
♦ *baking parchment*
♦ *small, sharp knife*
♦ *flour for dusting*
♦ *boiled sweets (candies)*
♦ *toothpick*
♦ *baking tray*
♦ *acrylic gesso*
♦ *paintbrushes*
♦ *gold craft paint*
♦ *acrylic satin (low luster) varnish*
♦ *fine gold cord*

1 Enlarge the templates provided and cut out. Roll out the dough on baking parchment to a thickness of 8mm/⅜in. Place a template on the dough and cut out using a sharp knife. Lightly dust the surface with flour and place a boiled sweet (candy) in the centre. Cut around it, adding a 2mm/¹⁄₁₆in margin. Remove the sweet and lift out the piece of dough.

2 Pierce a hole in the top of each shape with a toothpick. Transfer the models, on the parchment, to a baking tray and bake at 120°C/250°F/Gas ½ for 9 hours. Place a boiled sweet in each hole and return to the oven for 30 minutes, then set aside to cool.

3 Taking care not to paint the "stained glass" centre, undercoat the dough with acrylic gesso and allow to dry. Paint the dough with gold craft paint, then apply four coats of varnish. Hang the ornaments from gold cord.

Nutcracker Soldier

This smart fellow is modelled over a cardboard tube and has movable arms. He is based on a traditional wooden toy that was a great favourite in nineteenth-century Germany.

YOU WILL NEED
- *brown paper tape, scissors and ruler*
- *cardboard tube*
- *sheet of hard wooden board (to fit in oven), generously oiled*
- *salt dough*
- *rolling pin*
- *small, sharp knife*
- *skewer*
- *baking parchment and baking tray*
- *aluminium foil*
- *acrylic gesso*
- *paintbrushes*
- *acrylic or craft paints*
- *acrylic satin (low luster) varnish*
- *scraps of fur fabric*
- *all-purpose glue*
- *large-eyed needle and fine gold cord*

1 Cut lengths of brown paper tape in half lengthways and stick them over one end of the tube to cover it. Roll out the dough 8mm/⅜in thick. Place the tube on the wooden board and lay the dough over it. Tuck the dough around the tube and trim where it meets the board and at the top and base.

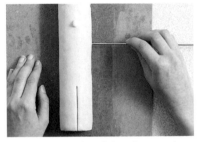

2 Press a circle of dough over the covered end of the tube and trim level with the side. Smooth the join. Mould a small triangle for the nose, moisten and press it on. Indent the division between the legs with the knife blade. Using a skewer, pierce a hole on each side, 8cm/3¼in below the top of the head.

4 Round the ends, then flatten the arms slightly and bend each into a curve. Indent the wrists, cuffs and epaulettes with a knife and pierce a hole below each epaulette. Transfer the pieces, on the parchment, to a baking tray and bake for 7 hours at 120°C/250°F/Gas ½.

3 On parchment, roll out some dough to 8mm/⅜in thick. Cut blocks 25 x 8mm/1 x ⅜in for the feet. Roll sausage arms, 1.5cm/⅝in thick and 8cm/3¼in long.

5 Turn the body over and support it with foil. Roll out some dough 8mm/⅜in thick and cover the back of the body, trimming the edges to fit. Smooth over the joins.

6 Return the model to the oven for another 4 hours. Stand the soldier upright and butt the feet up against the model, joining them with a little raw dough. Bake for another 1½ hours.

7 When cool, prime the body and arms with acrylic gesso, then paint the model as desired. Leave to dry. Apply four coats of varnish.

8 Cut strips of fur fabric for the hair and beard, cutting through the knitted backing fabric only. Glue in place.

9 Thread a large-eyed needle with fine gold cord and knot the ends tightly. Thread the needle through one arm, through the body and through the second arm. Fasten the cord against the second arm with a secure knot. Cut off the excess cord.

Animal Decorations

Create a menagerie of cheerful creatures to decorate your home during the festive season. Salt dough tree decorations were very popular in nineteenth-century Germany, and they are just as appealing today.

YOU WILL NEED
- ◆ *baking parchment*
- ◆ *pencil*
- ◆ *scissors*
- ◆ *salt dough*
- ◆ *rolling pin*
- ◆ *small, sharp knife*
- ◆ *ruler*
- ◆ *fruit corer*
- ◆ *drinking straw*
- ◆ *baking tray*
- ◆ *fine-grade sandpaper*
- ◆ *watercolour paints*
- ◆ *paintbrushes*
- ◆ *metallic craft paints*
- ◆ *acrylic satin (low luster) varnish*
- ◆ *ribbon*

1 Enlarge the templates provided and cut out. Roll out the dough on baking parchment to a thickness of 5mm/¼in and cut around the templates. Carefully indent the broken lines with the tip of a knife. Cut strips 5mm/¼in wide for the frames, using a ruler to keep the edges even. Moisten the edges of the plaques and position the strips, mitring the corners.

2 Place the pyramid and animal templates on the dough and cut out. Cut out the cheetah's head. Mould a diamond for the camel's ear. Moisten and press on to the head, indenting it with the knife tip. Moisten the cheetah's head and press it on to the body, overlapping the neck. Cut out a fin for the dolphin and a triangle for the cheetah's nose. Indent the facial features.

3 Cut four circles of dough with a fruit corer; use one for the sun on the cheetah plaque. Punch holes in the other three with a drinking straw and fix one to the top of each plaque. Transfer the pieces, on the parchment, to a baking tray and bake at 120°C/ 250°F/Gas ½ for 1 hour.

4 Moisten the undersides of the cut-out shapes and smear with dough. Moisten the plaques and press the pieces gently in position. Return them to the oven for another 9 hours. Allow to cool, then lightly sand the edges.

5 Paint the models with water-colour paints. Use a fine paint-brush to draw the stars on the camel plaque with metallic paint. Apply four coats of varnish, allowing the varnish to dry between coats. Thread ribbon through the rings to hang up the plaques.

Indian-style Ornaments

These finely detailed ornaments are inspired by traditional Indian decorative motifs. Decorate them with the brightest possible paints and inks to evoke the vivid colours of an Indian festival.

YOU WILL NEED
- *thin cardboard*
- *pencil*
- *scissors*
- *salt dough*
- *rolling pin*
- *baking parchment*
- *flour for dusting*
- *small, sharp knife*
- *toothpick*
- *drinking straw*
- *baking tray*
- *metal nail file*
- *acrylic gesso*
- *medium and fine paintbrushes*
- *metallic inks and fluorescent acrylic paints*
- *acrylic matt (flat) varnish*
- *scrap of green foil crêpe paper*
- *strong glue*
- *selection of small beads and sequins*

1 Copy the templates provided on to thin cardboard and cut out. Roll out the dough on baking parchment to 5mm/¼in thick. Place the templates on top and cut around each with a sharp knife. For the flower design, cut out the holes in the petals and emboss the central motif with the point of the knife.

2 Make the pricked patterns using a toothpick and a drinking straw. Make a hole in the top of each decoration for hanging.

3 Cut out the relief designs from dough and stick them to the moistened surface of the ornaments. Transfer all the pieces, on the baking parchment, to a baking tray and bake for 5 hours. Allow to cool.

4 File the edges smooth, then prime the designs with two coats of acrylic gesso. Paint the flower with lime green metallic ink, then paint inside the cut-outs with dark green. Add the fine details.

5 For the hand motif, paint all around the edges in bright pink paint. Paint the rest of the hand with orange acrylic paint and add fine details in pink and turquoise, using the embossed areas as a guide. Paint the paisley designs in your choice of colours.

6 Apply four coats of varnish to all the decorations. Allow to dry. To complete the hand, cut out a flower motif from a scrap of green foil crêpe paper and glue it down on to the palm of the hand. To complete the flower and paisley designs, stick on beads and sequins after painting the fine details in bright pink.

Court Jester

This flamboyant jester has a stuffed fabric body and head, hands and legs modelled from salt dough, in the style of old porcelain-headed figures. The weight of his head makes him loll in a fashion appropriate for a court buffoon.

You will need
- *aluminium foil*
- *masking tape*
- *2 small brass bells*
- *baking parchment*
- *salt dough*
- *small, sharp knife*
- *small cardboard tube*
- *cooking oil*
- *baking tray*
- *acrylic gesso*
- *paintbrushes*
- *acrylic or craft paints*
- *acrylic matt (flat) varnish*
- *tracing paper*
- *pencil*
- *scissors*
- *scraps of beige, red, blue and black fabric*
- *polyester wadding (batting)*
- *needle and matching thread*
- *all-purpose glue*
- *PVA (white) glue*
- *small gold beads*
- *mohair knitting wool*
- *gold cord*

1 Using aluminium foil, mould an egg shape 6cm/2⅜in high for the head. Roll two foil sausages 5cm/2in long for the hat, curving them and narrowing the tips into points. Stick them to the head with masking tape and tape a bell to each point.

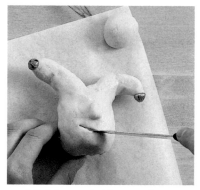

2 Working on baking parchment, smear a 5mm/¼in layer of dough over the front of the head and hat. Mould a small triangle for the nose and press in place. Smooth on a ball of dough for the chin. Use the point of a knife to cut the mouth.

3 Cut a cardboard tube in half lengthways and oil one half. Roll two 2.5cm/1in balls of dough for the hands. Flatten them over the tube. Cut a slit in each to make thumbs and pat the edges to round them. Attach small sausages for cuffs.

4 Roll two 2cm/¾in sausages of foil for the legs, 12.5cm/5in long. Bend 4cm/1½in of each up for the foot and squeeze the toe to a point. Cover the front of the leg and foot with dough, moulding the toe upwards to a point.

5 Transfer all the pieces, on parchment, to a baking tray and bake at 120°C/250°F/Gas ½ for 4 hours. Cover the rest of the head and legs with dough, remove the hands from the cardboard and return all the pieces to the oven for 3 hours.

6 Roll three 1.5cm/⅝in balls of dough, flatten them and press on to the base of the head and the tops of the legs. Return to the oven for 6 hours. Cool, then prime the legs and hat with acrylic gesso and paint with acrylic or craft paints. Apply four coats of varnish to all the pieces.

7 Use the templates at the back of the book to cut out two fabric body pieces. Stitch together with a 5mm/¼in seam allowance, leaving the arms, legs and neck open. Snip the curves, turn right side out and fill with polyester wadding (batting).

8 Stitch along the broken lines through all thicknesses. Turn under 5mm/¼in at the neck, arm and leg openings. Gather the folded neck edge with a running stitch, insert the head and pull up the threads tightly. Secure with glue. Repeat with the hands and legs.

▶

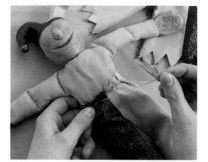

9 Using the templates, cut out a blouse and trousers in beige and red, a blue scarf and a black mask. On the wrong side, coat the jagged edges of the clothes and the whole of the mask with PVA (white) glue to prevent fraying. Leave to dry, then cut out.

10 Stitch the centre front and back seams of the blouse, leaving an opening at the back of the neck. Stitch the side seams and clip the curves. Fold the trouser sections in half with right sides together and stitch the inner leg seams. Clip the curves then join the trouser legs along the remaining seam. Turn right side out.

11 Sew a small gold bead to each point of the clothes, reinforcing the stitching with PVA (white) glue on the inside. Put on the trousers and stitch to the body. Put on the blouse and sew up the back seam. Fold under the neck edge and stitch to the body. Tie the scarf around the neck and secure with a little glue.

12 Gather the blouse and trousers at the wrists and knees. Draw up the threads tightly around the rims of the hands and legs and glue in place. Glue on some mohair wool for hair and glue on the mask. Tie a length of gold cord around the waist as a belt.

Templates

Sun Plaque p.28

Checkered Heart p.17

Traditional Wheatsheaf p.38

Animal Decorations p.52

Goddess Wall Plaque p.32

Fruit-filled Cornucopia p.40

Fish Plaque p.30

Flying Angel p.22

Jewelled Window Ornaments p.48

Traditional
Folk Angel p.45

Sponged Goose Keyrack p.42

Gingerbread Heart p.16

Indian-style Ornaments p.54

Court Jester p.56

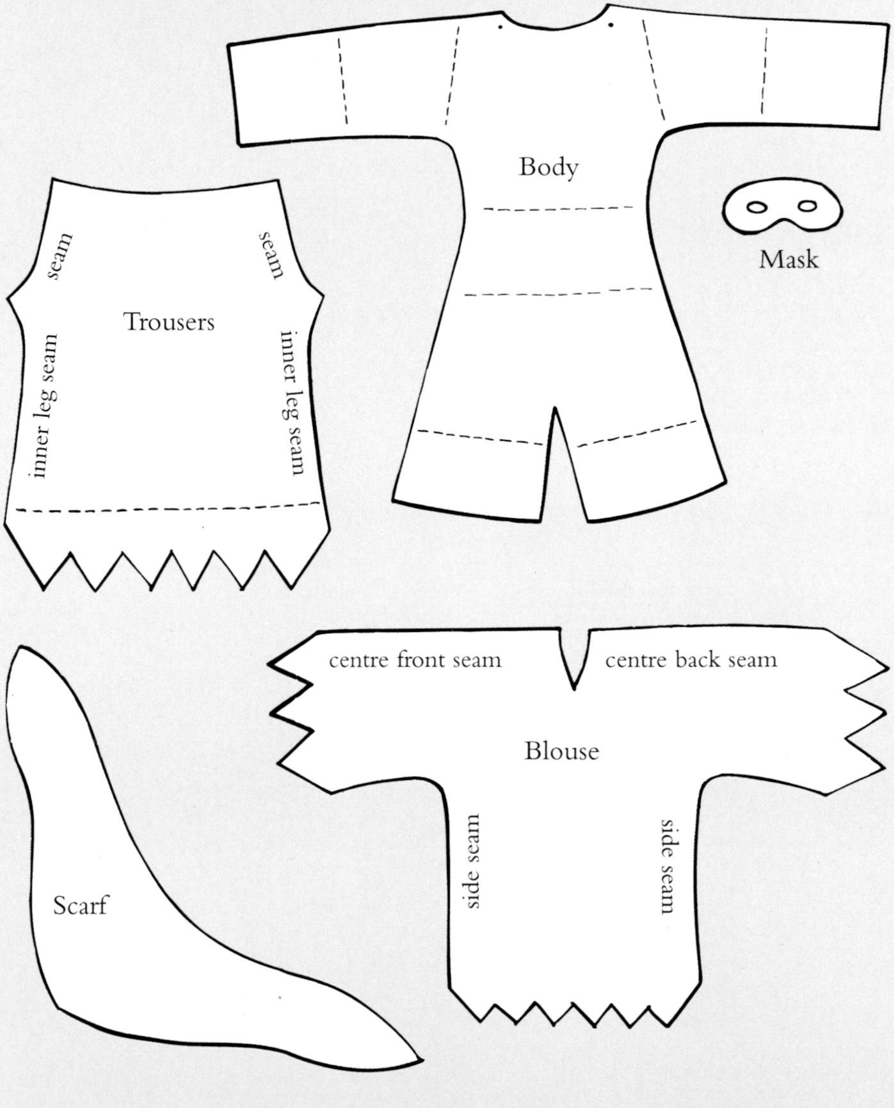

Body

Mask

Trousers

seam

seam

inner leg seam

inner leg seam

Scarf

centre front seam

centre back seam

Blouse

side seam

side seam

Index